The Twitter Blueprint

Build a massive following on Twitter the right way

Anita Doll Fiouris

DEDICATION

This work is dedicated to my amazing sons Kris, Alex and Nick and to my biggest fan, best friend, and husband, Andreas. These are the men in my life; the *"why"* for everything that I do.

CONTENTS

PREFACE

Revising this edition of The Twitter Blueprint has been a great learning experience. So many things have changed, not only on Twitter, but also on the Twitter applications that support many of the activities in regard to how Twitter operates within our Social Media Blueprint System. Due to the ripple effect from those changes, the system needed an overhaul - almost every one of the third party applications ("Cool Tools) used had to be changed. The Cool Tools listed in Chapter 3 are as of publish date – recommended.

Changes to all of the platforms of social media occur so frequently that determining when to time revisions and rewrites gets rather involved. Does one use a set time table or use an "as needed" method to schedule these inevitable and frequent revisions? If "as needed" is used - what parameters does one use to determine what a large enough change is? We have, to this point, vacillated between the two, and at the time this book heads off to print the jury, as they say, is still out!. Due to the above mentioned changes we no longer use Tweetspinner and have replaced it with *TweetAdder*, in case we've missed a minor reference to Tweetspinner, just replace it with TweetAdder.

It would be remiss of me not to mention how *The Social Media Blueprint System & "The Twitter Blueprint* book" were first conceived.

I will be forever grateful to Brad Hager and Susan Walsh for providing a forum and a game plan that allowed me to develop an easily duplicatable Social Media Optimization (SMO) system for any business interested in using social media as a part of their marketing strategy. During the Spring and Summer of 2009, a small group of entrepreneurs with considerably diverse practical business experience formed a mastermind group with the goal of dissecting and interpreting various aspects of an emerging phenomenon we now commonly call "social media". It was that research, and the knowledge gained that led to the inspiration and ultimately the creation of this regularly updated Book and *The Social Media Marketing Blueprint* that now serves hundreds of businesses all over the world.

Whether a traditional or home-based business, a political campaign, a charitable organization or cause – all that want to reach a larger audience to get a message out will benefit from the ground breaking work that of that mastermind group led by Brad Hager.

A special thanks to Mr. Jack Thomas for generously sharing his extensive knowledge on the subject of Twitter, ecommerce and SEO. Jack is an all around great guy; I highly recommend that you follow him on Twitter (@TexasJackFlash)!

Peace, Harmony, Laughter & Love (& happy tweeting)

Anita

1

WHAT IS TWITTER?

Using the most literal description, Twitter is a social networking and micro-blogging service that allows its users to send updates, as well as to read other users updates. These updates are in the form of text-based posts of up to 140 characters in length and referred to as *"tweets"*. Individuals using Twitter can see not only their own posts, but also the posts of others that they have chosen to "follow" and the follower's followers. This is similar to the "friending" relationships on Facebook, yet with one very important distinction, an individual on Twitter does not need to have permission to be a follower or someone following another. In other words, this is an open platform – it does not have an opt-in requirement. That distinction is the first reason that Twitter was chosen as part of the complete *Social Media Marketing Blueprint* that I developed early in 2009.

This revolutionary Web 2.0 micro-blogging platform has definitely made itself known in a very short time, quite literally, all over the world. Communication across the globe has gotten easier, faster and much cheaper almost overnight. With the addition of developments within the world of mobile technology and *Smart Phones*, Twitter wisely made sure they were in the game - early. As a result, from 2009 – 2010, Twitter's enjoyed a growth rate of 368% rivaling only the growth of Facebook.

Twitter grows so consistently and rapidly that the only thing constant with it, is it is ever evolving and changing. Its popularity and its both rapid and sustained growth have allowed for the creation of a rather large cottage industry with literally thousands of various applications and software compatible to make Tweeting more convenient, mobile and fun. These applications, too, are necessarily ever evolving and adapting to the constantly moving world of not only Twitter but also that of social media as a whole. The best advice for a newly hatched peep (AKA: a Twitter novice) is to adopt an attitude that change and the resulting challenges are the norm. In this way the "Twitterverse" is more like a swiftly flowing stream than a tranquil meadow. As an obscure military General has been quoted to have said, "You may not like change, but you will like obsolescence even less." To save your sanity and to have as much fun as possible here I suggest that you think of this as an adventure!

Welcome to the party!

When attempting to understand how those that achieve the most benefit from this fast paced social media platform behave while on Twitter, an analogy is useful: Twitter is like a very large cocktail party! As you walk through the mass of guests you can hear many different conversations on many different topics all happening at the same time (your twitstream).

Let's take a minute and imagine that you are a guest at the most important social event of the year. You will come across a few people you already know but most are friends that you haven't met yet. Of course, this means that you will want to make look your best. This is not the time to show off your skills at burping the alphabet while wearing raggedy clothes. It is **very important** to make certain that your profile page shows your professional persona. You will also want to get involved with positive, like-minded people that are interested in whatever your target market is interested in. Next you will want to participate in lively, interesting conversations with those individuals thus developing a good relationship with many.

Research has shown that the best way to engage others on Twitter is to provide them with information they feel is valuable as well as interesting to them. Basically, the majority of the 140 character conversation needs to be mostly about them, their interests and needs - at least 80% of the time. Once you are perceived as one that uplifts and contributes to others (as well as to the whole group), then it is just fine to mention your business, site, service, product (whatever it is that you are on Twitter to promote), As you may have already realized, to get the most benefit from Twitter the real secret to success, as in life, is in building relationships. Doing so makes it easier to meet new and interesting people. Using twitter with this mindset will quickly make you the life of the party and people will begin enjoying your tweets, follow you, tell others and recommend that they follow you – and that is a *very* good thing!

"Twit-speak"

As commonly happens within a specific profession, group or class, where people communicate within a very specific field of endeavor or activity, certain words or phrases develop a meaning all their own. Some common examples are the Computer/Technology world ; the sports world, etc. Twitter is no different and has developed a vocabulary of its own. To make it easier and more fun to understand the world of Twitter, a short, but by no means complete review of some of the most common (and most confusing) terms follows:

Tweet: a text based post with a maximum of 140 characters that answers the question (located on the top of your Twitter page) "What are you doing?" or better put "What are you thinking?" Millions of tweets are made every day from people all over the world using an ever growing number of devices to Tweet. Everything is discussed in these short posts from an inspiring original observation, to a great quote, to the latest news, to the launch of a new business or product, to where someone is planning to go for lunch.

Peeps or Tweeple: People that participate (have accounts and use them) on Twitter. Basically, this means you, your target audience and the other 140 million+ users out there!

Twitstream/Twitterverse: The conversations that are on Twitter at any given time. The entire stream is *huge*. The part that you will actually see and participate in is just your portion of the whole Twitstream and will grow as your account grows with more and more Following and Followers.

Following: You choose the individuals that you will be following. That means that their tweets (posts) will appear in your twitstream. This is where we will target specific people to begin following. Niche and target leaders here are key in following. Reciprocity is also very important with who you follow (see below)

Followers: These are the people that have chosen to follow you. Your posts show up in their twitstream. These people find you and become your followers in different ways. In the beginning of developing your sphere of influence here, we will concentrate on the reciprocity of those that you are following (again, see below). Thus they become a follower. Your follower count is how your Twitter market reach is determined. The larger the follower number the more potential listeners you have. This is the segment we will focus on growing, both in targeted numbers, influence (and many other quality factors discussed later).

2

WHY WOULD BUSINESSES USE TWITTER?

As mentioned in Chapter One, Twitter does not have an approval process for someone to become a part of your sphere of influence. Thus, creating a large sphere has fewer restrictions than other "opt – in" type platforms. There is another characteristic of most social media platforms, including Twitter that adds to the market appeal to any savvy business owner. It is that these platforms allow anyone to communicate with anyone else located anywhere in the world for free - provided both have internet access. That seemingly small capability allows a completely different level of social interaction to occur on a global scale. Communication is now convenient, mobile, fast, global and most importantly cheap (if not free). If you pause and reflect on this for a minute, you will begin to see the potential power and possible uses of Twitter for anyone (including businesses) are limited only by the imagination. Individuals, groups (political, civic, or religious) as well as businesses can now reach a much larger audience and get their message across with less investment of time and money than ever before. The playing field of communicating a message to the world has been leveled. An additional benefit is that their target audience is "tuned in" to them and "listening" if not communicating directly, all for a fraction of the cost! No one knows exactly how many people across the world use twitter daily and Twitter isn't telling. Statistics from the last part of 2010 show that Twitter had a minimum of 140 million daily direct users. That means all of the millions of power Tweeters that use third party tools such a *Hootsuite, TweetDeck* and the list goes on and on with new applications popping up almost weekly. Suffice it to say that the number of Tweeters is growing daily at a rate that astonishes even the experts. As mentioned earlier, from 2009 - 2010 the number of Twitter users grew 368%.

Soon after its inception, online entrepreneurs and other tech savvy businesses seized the opportunity to generate leads with this new forum. Since then, the word has spread like wild fire and twitter has fast become a favorite for generating free leads in the internet marketing world. Twitter continues to be one of the major means for communicating in real time with new prospects, business partners and customers going forward. As of today, there doesn't appear to be a slowdown in sight.

Since the first edition of The Twitter Blueprint went into circulation, I have heard basically the same objection from business owners as well as individuals asking "why twitter". The basis of the objection is this, Twitter isn't personal enough, and that it is hard, if not impossible to develop a relationship in 140 characters or less. My favorite reply to this complaint is that it would indeed seem to be the case, yet 1 out of 8 couples married in 2009, met on social media! ;-) Now that I have their and your attention, we do need to take a look at Twitter's role. Twitter is best used as one of the tools (albeit a very important one) you need to use to get your message out to the marketplace.

I want to explain why Twitter needs to be an integral part of any Social Media marketing campaign. Let's start with an example; you have a business / service / product / candidate / idea that you want to promote using social media. You have your Facebook profile and a business fan page and have had moderate success with beginning relationships with potential clients /consumers on both your personal profile and your fan page. You may even have a great blog and a fantastic website. If you need to build a list of people that are interested in your message, how do you make contact? Now the question becomes: *'how do I let people know that what I've created is here?"* You've got the content, it's just that you need more exposure to the masses within your target market. Remember, marketing, promoting or sales (of any kind) is really a numbers game; you need to have as many people as possible interacting with you online. Here's an example to clarify my point, let's say you have 4,000 friends on facebook. Your conversion rate (that's the percentage of people that gravitate to what you are promoting) is 10%. That is out of the 4,000 friends, 400 people will go to look at what you offer - with me so far? The more people you can reach, the more that 10% will be.

Well, Facebook has VERY strict rules that govern how many people you can ask to be your friend or to come "like" your fan page. These guidelines are not well defined – yet, when you receive a warning from Facebook regarding "friending rules" it is wise to heed that warning! Unlike Twitter, Facebook will permanently shut down an account for little reason and you have very little recourse, if any.

Well, here is the challenge – How do you get vast numbers of people within your reach of Facebook (or anywhere else for that matter) quickly and easily, when you are not a celebrity, with all of the rules that facebook has on "friending" people, not to mention the very drastic method used to enforce those rules. Put another way, how do we get around that pesky friending rule and keep our account at the same time? You also don't want to appear to others, who you want to befriend, to be desperate - you'd like to keep your dignity.

So what can you do – for free? The best answer is one word –**_Twitter_**! How is Twitter a solution to the "friending" challenge Facebook presents? Easy, there are NO Facebook restrictions on how many people can ask **_you_** to be **_their_** friend! The people from Twitter are requesting your friendship! That is, of course, because we set it up that way and invited them to do just that! Remember the analogy of the cocktail party in Chapter one? That analogy provided an illustration for how to develop your brand on Twitter, your persona, a perspective in which to interact with others.

When discussing the function of Twitter in getting a message out to others another analogy is useful: Think of Twitter as the world's largest billboard on the most used road in the world and everyone travels at 140 characters. People are moving past and have the opportunity to see your image. Then, if something entices them enough, they will take the time to learn more about you, your message, product or business. Twitter simply gives them the message that you exist, a quick glance at what you are about and a way to connect in another arena.

In the early days of working with Twitter, I used to think of the traditional sales funnel with the wide top of the funnel to help direct prospects through the sales process as an example. Yet, with more experience (successes and failures) I feel the billboard analogy is more accurate. There is a very important aspect to Twitter that makes neither analogy completely fit. Let's consider that your potential prospects are in the global population or in your local vicinity passers-by take a quick look and decide if they want to know more. Those that do, have a way to conveniently learn more and you are on your way to creating a relationship. Here's the difference, while they are looking at you and forming a judgment, you are looking at them in the same way! What a new concept – being able to prune out those you don't want into the smaller part of your sales funnel. That is where Twitter (as well as most other platforms for social media) is most useful. You can target who you allow to see your short, quick statements that would be of interest to your target market and thus let your great personality show through. You are able to target the who by selecting those that you follow by what they have in their profile information and biographical information that they put there. This is made faster and easier with third party applications that are available, we discuss those in greater detail in Chapter 3.

People that are "open" will naturally gravitate to find out more about you. That is if you've set up your profile properly, as we described in Chapter 1. That is where you have the first opportunity to develop a relationship – no matter how superficial the connection is, you are in control.

So why would businesses flock to Twitter? (Yep, the pun was intentional!) Let me answer the question with a question. "Where else can a business communicate on a global scale with actively participating prospects within their target market; have little to no restrictions on reaching that target market and the monetary cost is infinitesimal when compared to traditional methods of marketing?" Now you can see what is meant when people keep saying that social media, in this case Twitter, has leveled the playing field for small businesses. Previously corporations with marketing departments were the only real players. The playing field may be level – for now. I don't expect that to remain the case for long. Whenever a new development or industry appears in the marketplace eventually a pecking order gets established. It's best to be in during the early developmental stages.

3

WHAT ARE THE COOLEST TOOLS?

As I stated earlier, an entire cottage industry has popped up to provide software, applications and other such handy tools to use with Twitter. Currently there are over 2,500 such third party applications. As in the industry these companies serve, this is an area where change is the norm. Out of necessity, these tools must constantly stay current with Twitter. There are three major types of changes: First, like many new business ventures they come and go. They are here today and gone tomorrow. A second rather common phenomenon, some applications are "free" early on, once popular they begin to charge a fee. A third tendency we've noticed is that what works for awhile doesn't work in the same capacity later. A change on Twitter renders the application obsolete and no one has created a "fix". Be aware, not all of the applications that you find on the web are useable. Those that are may, not be useable for you and your marketing needs forever.

The best example is the "unfollowing" change that went into effect during 2010. The 2 most important tools we used in the Blueprint system at that time to monitor the following / follower ratio was Tweetspinner and Karma. These were useful for several of the steps within the Blueprint System – most importantly – unfollowing and purging. Once Twitter notified all third party applications that they would get booted off – have no access to their twitter API – every application that had previously had an unfollow feature either disappeared, as in the case of Karma, or shut that feature down, as did Tweetspinner. As you will soon see, unfollowing those that do not reciprocate (follow you back once you follow them) is vital to break the magical glass ceiling. Twitter's 2,000 following restriction ends once an account has 2,000 followers – that's the glass ceiling. Having people you are following that don't understand the concept of reciprocation and don't follow you is not helping you in any way – not only in breaking that 2,000 follower barrier but they are also not interested in the give and take of communication, thus won't be of much value to you later as prospective clients/consumers.

Obviously, you can imagine our predicament when we were no longer able to clear out the deadwood in our twitter stream! Following, with no ability to unfollow efficiently, thus came to a standstill. It was simply too cumbersome to look up each individual profile to see if they were following us back and if not, to "unfollow" each – one by one. The good news, is that after much trial and error, we discovered an application that found a way to overcome the unfollow/purge challenge and then some! Our system was able to move again! Keep this example in mind when the next round of changes hit and there are hitches with the tools use are using – it's just part of the deal! Some practical advice: Don't allow yourself to get too frustrated, and stay connected to others in the field. While, there are many benefits to being involved at the beginning of any enterprise, there are times when it can feel like a double edged sword!

Before getting bogged down in learning all of these tools, here is the best way for a new Twitter user to benefit from what each of these third party sites has to offer.

1. The **background sites** will be useful early on to get your account set up and looking snazzy right away. Once that's done, you will not be visiting these much.

2. **Twitter Self Listing Sites**, put your twitter accounts on *WeFollow* and *Twellow*. Use this mainly to find who to "mimic" follow within the categories that would most likely be where your target audience would be. The other benefit is that anyone looking for those on Twitter within a specific category will find you (if you listed yourself)

3. The **automation tools** URL tracking tools plus TweetDeck and *TweetAdder*. While in the category of automation each runs completely different function and each is valuable if you are serious about obtaining a massive following fast. TweetAdder's 24/7 capability allows a user to preset and automate: tweets, who to follow, who to unfollow, who to follow back, what to DM.

Tip: *running SMO on less than 90 minutes a week (once you have it up and running) would not be possible without TweetAdder!*

4. **Ranking Sites** measure how you're doing along the way so that you can tweak activity to be as effective and efficient as possible. While important, these won't be useful until after you've been tweeting awhile.

Background Sites:
Tools to get your Twitter account looking it's best!

We've all know about "dressing for success" and heard that "you never have a second chance to make a first impression". When considering the look of your Twitter account, remember branding. Your twitter account should have the same visual impact that your other sites have and needs to stand out from the , quite literally, millions of other twitter accounts out there. You can do this with your profile photo and the individualized background you choose.

To make these changes simply choose the Settings option from the drop down menu located in the upper right corner when logged into your twitter account. When in Settings, you go to Profile, to customize your profile picture and personalize your bio information. Next you choose "Design" to upload your customized background and make corresponding changes to the rest of the color scheme on your account. As always, don't forget to save your changes before you leave the page!

The following sites, MyTweetSpace, TwitBacks and TwitrBackgrounds, are just a few of the many sites that let you personalize your twitter profile page. I chose these for two reasons: first, for the option to use your own photo as part of the background, the second, the option of free backgrounds - free is always good! Play around and let your personality shine through. The better your profile page looks, the better quality Tweeple you will attract to follow you!

MyTweetSpace.com

"Personalized Twitter Backgrounds" $4.88

Personalize your profile with a custom badge. Add your name, logo, website and more. 100's of great designs. Get your Personalized Background Today!

Get Started!

TwitBacks.com

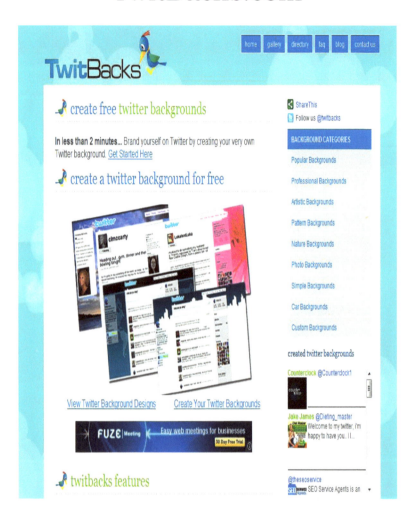

TwitrBackgrounds.com

Self Listing Sites
Get listed on the "Yellow Pages" for Twitter

They are free and you get to classify yourself according to what your target audience will be looking for. There are several of these type of classification sites, we recommend the two most popular, Twellow and WeFollow because that is where you'll most likely been seen by your audience. Both are user powered Twitter directories, yet each with slightly different approaches. Both are useful and it is recommended that you be sure to use both.

This means that as soon as you have your account set up properly, register yourself on each *Twellow* and *WeFollow*. Again, these are like the Twitter Yellow Pages, it's important that you take advantage of this free method to put yourself in front of your target market, especially those that are actively looking for Tweeple that do what you do. Be sure to carefully think through the categories that you choose.

Twellow is a directory of public Twitter accounts, with hundreds of categories and search features to help you find people who matter to you. Registering with *Twellow* will allow you to update your *Twellow* profile and categories, add links to your other social media profiles, create an extended bio with whatever information and links you would like to add, and easily follow other Twitter users right from *Twellow*!

WeFollow is quite literally an online directory with little to no fluff. Its genius is in its straight forward categories and classifications.

Twellow.com

WeFollow.com

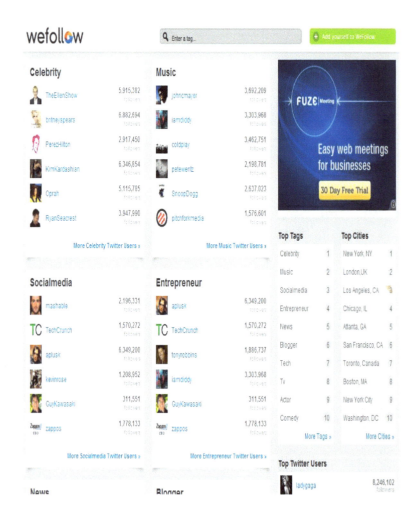

Automation Tools –
3 subcategories:
(1) Track, (2) Manage (3) Automate

1. Track your clicks...

...and shorten them at the same time! With only 140 characters to work with, you will soon get great at reducing! These tools are great for trimming long URLs. Most importantly they are very useful for tracking various statistics about each URL that you shrink. Statistics such as the number of visits (or click thrus) your URL has over time via various sites, Twitter being one of them, are valuable in determining the effectiveness of various campaigns.   I recommend that you visit each one and get a feel for how it operates and see for yourself what it tracks. One will stand out as fitting your unique needs better than others. There is also nothing wrong with using more than one site, especially while you are getting used to this, after all it is free!

We will discuss the importance of tracking later in the *"Measure how you are doing"* section of this chapter.

BudUrl.com

Bit.ly

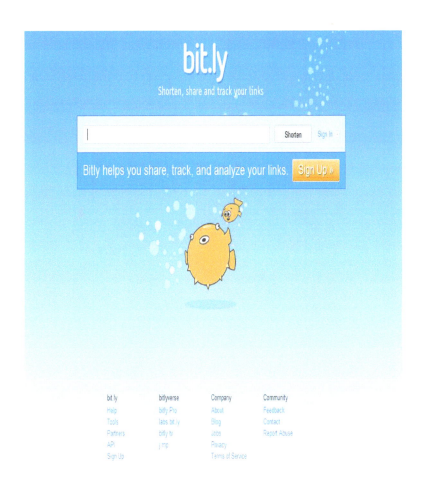

Tr.im

2. Manage, Simplify, Organize

TweetDeck: One "dashboard" to rule them all! Okay, it's supposed to be "ring" as in the Lord of the Rings! Seriously, we promised easy and efficient - this is it, at least once you get used to it. *TweetDeck* is software that you will download onto your computer to help you manage Twitter (great when you have more than 1 account). It organizes your tweets and allows you to re-tweet, mention, DM and more with just the click of your mouse. It will even allow you to communicate on Facebook from the one easy dashboard. You can see everything that is going on in your Twitstream, organize columns to fit your needs, set the options to show how many followers those that show up in your stream have – all at the same time. Remember, this is downloaded to your computer. Once it's loaded, open it by clicking the icon located on your desktop. Be sure to take the tutorials and follow the advice on "getting started". As you will see on *TweetDeck*.com: *TweetDeck* is your personal real-time browser, connecting you with your contacts across Twitter, Facebook, MySpace, LinkedIn, Foursquare, Google Buzz and more.

The best advice we can give for you to get up and moving quickly on TweetDeck is to take the tutorials and just do it. One thing you need to do – in "Options", choose to show the number of followers in Tweets. This will let you know the clout of the individual that is tweeting. And will let you decide whether to interact and how to respond to them.

TweetDeck.com

3. Automation: secret to it all!

Tweet Adder is the tool that anyone serious about managing a twitter account effectively and efficiently must have. It is also the only "cool tool" that is not free. There is a one-time charge with free updates. This is the one tool that is running on my computer 24 hours a day,365 days a year. Just set it and go!

TweetAdder describes itself like this:
Automate Twitter Promotion and Marketing -Find and Engage in Like-Minded Twitter Followers and Automate Twitter Posts! That's right! We have added every benefit imaginable. All bells and whistles included! Everything you need to automatically grow your network and profit on autopilot.

Filters in both Tweet Search and Profile Data Search:

- Keyword
- Location
- Recency
- Language spoken
- Ability to remove profiles with default picture

Automated Tweet Search: Locates users to follow who tweeted a matching filter or keyword. Example Searches include (combine to form more complex searches)

- containing a word: twitter
- Containing multiple words: twitter marketing
- Negation: twitter -marketing
- Exact phrase: "twitter marketing"
- OR: twitter OR tweets

- Containing a hash tag: #twitter
- Not From a user: -from:username
- To a user: to:username
- Mentioning a user: @username

Profile Data Search: search twitter bio, plus filters

Location Search search by geographic location around the world, plus filters.

Twitter List Search imports another users twitter list.

Followers of a User obtains a list of profiles following a particular user.

Followed by a User obtains a list of profiles a user is following.

Multiple Twitter Account Management: You can manage more than one twitter profile. This will multiply your twitter networking spread out amongst several different twitter profiles. You can also manage advertising and public relations client's profiles as a twitter service.

Run Multiple Profiles Concurrently: Select as many of your profiles as you wish, and the software will run through each account automatically and complete your automated tasks with one instance of the software open!

Automated Following Features:

- Never follow the same person twice
- Special Blacklist to block following to specific people
- Auto Follow Twitter Users – Fully Control Twitter following with Follower Ratio, Max # of follows per day
- Auto Follow Stop Feature – Automatically stops when Twitter follow limits are reached

- Random Time Delay Settings- You choose what time intervals between follows, unfollows, tweets, and direct messages

Automated UnFollowing Features:

- Ability to unfollow ALL except your personal WHITELIST
- Auto Unfollow Twitter Users: Unfollow by #, follower to follow ratios, users who do not follow back with time frames
- Safe White List: Create a list of twitter users to never unfollow

Automatic Tweet helps you to keep your twitter profiles active, engaging, and interesting to keep your followers from leaving you. You can set up a multitude of tweets in the software, and allow the software to spread them out throughout the day

Automated Tweet Features

- Automated Tweets post throughout the day
- Post Tweets to Facebook, Linkedin, and Myspace!!
- Unique Tweet Generator – creates unique tweets automatically
- RSS Tweets – tweets any RSS feed whether from your blog updates, or any other source
- @Reply Tweets – post a random tweet @someone who posts a tweet directed @you
- Re-Tweets- Automatically re-tweet another user
- Mp3 Poster – Bands and artists can upload Mp3s to www.mp3twit.com and share on twitter
- Post Tweets with random time delay

Automate Direct Messages

Good for informing your followers of upcoming events, conferences, or any items you need to keep your followers informed about. Communicate with your followers automatically. No problem! Set your pre set messages to tweet, and your auto dm's to send messages to new followers welcoming them and go on your way!

- Thank you Direct Messaging – sends messages to your new followers
- Standard Direct Messaging – Sends messages to your followers

TweetAdder.com

Ranking Sites
Measure how you are doing!

To gauge the impact of any activity in business is important. From that information, we determine what activities are efficient, and what ones need to be tweaked or pitched out. All of the sites listed here are useful to help you track your Twitter Statistics as well as look up those of others. We recommend familiarizing yourself with all three. Eventually, you will gravitate to the one (or ones) that best fits you and your specific needs.

They can tell you how many people you reach in Twitter and exactly when you need to be active to reach them. Tracking the different metrics, from these various sites help you decide which measures are right for you and which are meaningful for your business. The information gained from sites like these give you dozens of ways to visualize your progress, thus helping you understand your social media efforts for your company.

The rating and ranking sites won't be of much value to you right away other than as sources of information on what it is they use to determine how they rank accounts – their metrics. After you've been up and running several weeks, then drop by and see how you're doing!

We will discuss more about clout, generosity, velocity, reach and other metrics tools in Chapter eight.

TwitterCounter.com

Twitalyzer.com

Twitalyzer knows who is in your social network and **we know where they live,** allowing you to be more targeted in your outreach efforts.

Get started with Twitalyzer and improve your targeting

Enter a Twitter username and click "Twitalyze!" | Twitalyze! | Sign In

Paid Plans

Twitalyzer offers three different pricing and service levels to suit the specific the needs of your social business.

Select a Plan!

Free Benchmarks

Twitalyzer provides Twitter's most robust benchmark reporting, ranking Twitter users ten different ways.

View Benchmarks

Recent Announcements from Twitalyzer

» Social Media is not a Game
» Thoughts on "Thought Leadership"
» Twitalyzer and Klout
» Welcome to Twitalyzer 4.0
» Upcoming changes effective January 2011

Read more in the Twitalyzer Blog!

Subscription Options · Blog · Feedback & Support · Contact Us

Twitalyzer is Copyright 2011 Twitalyzer, LLC and is a product of Web Analytics Demystified, Inc.

Twitaholic.com

The Twitaholic.com Top 100 Twitterholics based on Followers

#	Name (Screen Name)	Location	URL	Followers	Following	Updates	Joined
1	Lady Gaga (ladygaga)	New York, NY	http://www.ladygaga.com	8223452	144767	805	35 months ago
2	Justin Bieber (justinbieber)	on the MY WORLD TOUR!!!	http://www.youtube.com/justin...	7368664	107466	7654	23 months ago
3	Britney Spears (britneyspears)	Los Angeles, CA	http://www.britneyspears.com	6851217	415993	601	29 months ago
4	Barack Obama (BarackObama)	Washington, DC	http://www.barackobama.com	6669204	703408	1266	46 months ago
5	ashton kutcher (aplusk)	Los Angeles, California	http://www.facebook.com/Ashton	6347107	615	6462	25 months ago
6	Kim Kardashian (KimKardashian)	on a plane...	http://kimkardashian.celebuzz...	6332056	125	6834	23 months ago
7	Ellen DeGeneres (TheEllenShow)	California	http://www.ellentv.com	5900271	43996	3861	31 months ago
8	Katy Perry (katyperry)	Underneath a palm tree...	http://www.katyperry.com	5742864	68	2834	24 months ago
9	taylorswift13 (taylorswift13)		http://twitter.com/taylorswift13	5307373	50	1692	27 months ago
10	Oprah Winfrey (Oprah)	Chicago, IL	http://www.oprah.com	5107995	21	163	26 months ago
11	Shakira (shakira)	Bahamas	http://www.shakira.com	4409185	36	1751	21 months ago

4

WHAT IS THE GLASS CEILING?

Before we get too far ahead of ourselves, we need to discuss a hurdle that you will need to cross as soon as you can. It is the first obstacle in using Twitter effectively for business. This barrier is affectionately known as the glass ceiling. Twitter has set an obstacle in your path to generating a huge list of followers. Here is how it works: Twitter limits you to following only 2000 people until you have 2,000 followers. The limit of following 2000 people will be lifted when you have 2000 followers (people following you). After that, your following will be restricted to about 10% over the number of your followers. This is by no means an exact equation, for obvious reason Twitter doesn't provide exact details on the following barriers to stay one step ahead of the ever present bots and spammers.

To hit the 2000 follower threshold, you must be sure that you are sticking to the *Reciprocity Code* also known as the **Mutual Follow code** - *if people don't follow us back, we delete them*. This is when **Unfollowing** and **Purging** becomes vital! For that (and many other things that will automate your Twitter activity, we recommend an application called ***TweetAdder***). I recommend that when using *TweetAdder*, set the unfollow automated settings to unfollow all non-reciprocating accounts after 1 day, rather than the 3 day that comes pre-set on the program. After you have passed through the glass ceiling, then you can loosen those settings some. Though with over 300,000+ followers on multiple accounts, I haven't loosened mine up!

In order to better explain the need to unfollow, let me give you an example: Let's say someone has 1,999 people the he/she is following. Yet, this same person only has 130 people as followers. He will not be allowed to follow any more than 2,000 until more people choose to follow him. Why? Well, if this person isn't getting people to follow him, Twitter reasons that he must not be contributing to the Twitterverse and probably is just a spammer. So, this person's following is frozen until others in the Twitterverse feel he is giving valuable content to Twitter and follow him.

Here is how one breaks the glass ceiling: when you get to 1,800 people that you are following, purge the dead wood and small potatoes from your following list. If after 24 hours someone is not reciprocating (following you back), purge them. If you are sticking to the Mutual Follow code, that is, if people don't follow us back, we delete them - you'll break through the ceiling without a problem! Again, using the automated

TweetAdder settings, and manually pushing some unfollows through at least once or twice each day will help you achieve this quickly and easily.

Once you pass the 2,000 follower threshold– you will be limited to Twitter's 10% rule. This is a VERY vague rule, so don't get bogged down in the actual numbers. It works like this: If you have 2,560 followers, Twitter will only let you have 10% more following or 2,816 following (2,560 + 256 = 2,816). Again, purging (unfollowing) those that don't reciprocate within 24 to 48 hours is a good idea Please note that the White List (those that you don't ever want to purge) and Black List (those that you never want in either your following or followers list) become more and more important as your network on Twitter grows. Be sure to use this feature from the beginning to save yourself the time of loading on a large number of Tweeple later on.

.

5

HOW TO BUILD A MASSIVE FOLLOWER COUNT

Thus far we have discussed what Twitter is all about; the Twitter terms and phrases you will need to understand; what tools you will need and even some of the barriers. *Now for the fun stuff!*

"Luck favors the prepared"

First of all you want to open an account with twitter - *properly*. For your username, it is best to use a real name, yours or that of your business. Most people would rather follow a real person instead of something generic and embarrassingly spammy like "MrBigBucks". If your business name is too large or is already taken, go for a name that describes a benefit or a function. Be prepared to play around a bit! Stay away from tacky, spammy sounding names.

Next, put a good looking picture of you, most often a head shot is best or your logo as the Profile picture. Customize the rest of your account by playing around with the background and the color schemes. (Hint:

think branding) Using *MyTweetSpace.com, TwitterBackground.com and TwitBacks.com* will help you to:

- distinguish yourself from the crowd,
- attract your target market,
- solidify your brand
- and find your niche.

The good news here is that as you get more familiar with Twitter, you can change the look of your profile as often as you like! As for your online bio, you want to include a benefit statement or something that says people will learn something and enjoy following you, sprinkle in a few keywords, and make it positive and personal. Remember, the key here is to make it about serving your target market's needs.

As you see other bio's that you like, you will get more ideas about what you want yours to say, and you can always edit yours later to make changes.

As you start to build your followers list, keep in mind that this is about relationships with people – the right people. Be yourself and be authentic. In building relationships, you need to "give" in order to "get". You will want to actively listen to and share on a platform where they can learn about you as a human, where they can get to know you better. Facebook works great, if your websites aren't yet up and running. This builds a feeling of a trusting relationship. Once they perceive your content as valuable to themselves and others, they will begin to see you as an asset to their business and that you add value to their life in general. That is when they will be most open to join your mailing lists, buy your products/service, or look at your business venture. Interesting sometimes funny and positive light hearted conversations seem to work the best. Learning about those you are speaking with and giving back to them in the form of good content is critical – even if it's just a nice quote or a link to a video on YouTube that will make them smile.

Yet, keep an eye on the clock while on any social media site, especially Twitter. What I mean by that is find a way for quick interactions. Twitter can quickly become addictive and you don't want social media to become a time drain!

Don't just send people to your business capture/sales page or website straight from Twitter. Let them find out more about you – they will find their way into your business. ***Never forget the old (and very true) saying: "Everyone likes to buy; No one likes to be sold!"*** ☺

6

WHAT DO I TWEET ABOUT
& WHERE DO I FIND IT?

Okay, you want to be authentic and have interesting things to tweet – where do you find all of this valuable content? It really is easier than it seems at first. Find a subject that interests you, more often than not, your interest will come through and it will be interesting to others! More good news, the internet has an endless supply of information just waiting for you to discover! Relax, enjoy and stay positive in your tweets! Set aside a regular block of time each week to search for content at first. People love being around enthusiastic positive confident people. Here is a quick list of things I have used for content:

➤ Google Search: search "quote" (or "quotes") and whatever subject you like – leadership, life, love, humor, inspiration, perseverance. The best part is when you find something you like, simply copy and paste it where you want it!

➢ http://quotationspage.com: another great source for quotes from famous people.

➢ http://www.YouTube.com: great source for short video clips on any subject

➢ http://blip.fm: If you enjoy music this free site lets you become your own DJ and tweet (they call it "blip") out your favorite songs straight from that site with the click of the mouse!

Experiment with different things to see what it is that gets you the most re-tweets. As you can see you are limited only by your imagination, again just like in life!

.

7

NOW THAT YOU'RE READY, GO GET FOLLOWERS!

This is where we start having some fun with all of the information that you've learned so far! Keep in mind that *targeted following* is what we are doing here. So we will use the keywords, mimic follow within categories, tweet search following , and if applicable, geographic location searches. Don't let all of that fool you - it is an amazingly simple three-step process to building your Follower count! I will explain each step and give guidelines on how to make it happen via TweetAdder.

1. **Start Following** –When using TweetAdder, first you must build your *"To Follow List"* – do so with steps A through C found below. Once the list is built, move to the *"Follow/Unfollow Users"* section on TweetAdder. Set your parameters for automated activity and don't forget to click the *"automate"* button at the top. If doing this manually, you can follow people directly from either *Wefollow* or *Twellow*. Repeat

46

all three parts of this step until you are following a minimum of 250 people per day.

A. Use *Twellow* and *Wefollow* to find people that already have a large following in the categories that your target market would either be in or would be following - follow these category leaders. Keep these names handy so you can include them in part B below.

B. Select some of the highest ranked people in *Twellow* and *Wefollow* and enter their twitter id names into the *"Followers of a User"* section of *TweetAdder*. Click *"Search Now"*; this is where the magic of *TweetAdder* kicks in! Following those that are followers of an account listed in your chosen categories is called *"mimic following."*

C. Choose 3 - 5 keywords that would most likely be in the profile bios of your target market. Enter those (one at a time) into the *"Profile Data Search"* section on *TweetAdder*. Click *"Search Now"*. Keep doing this until you have exhausted all of the keywords. If your business is geographic specific, do the same for location section. Now your list of people to follow includes more of your target market!

2. **Begin tweeting** your witty and interesting content. Find the interesting tweets from your

twitter stream and re-tweet them. Be sure to thank those that re-tweet you or mentioned you. Make contact with others through Mentions or Re-tweets at least 25 times each day. This is where *TweetDeck* will be *very* valuable as a time saver. When using *TweetAdder* for automated tweeting, be sure to uncheck the *"Recurring Tweets"* section. (Repeating the same Tweet will get you shut down on Twitter surprisingly fast!) The easiest way to load Tweets onto *TweetAdder* is to create a notepad document with 1 tweet per line. Then import them onto *TweetAdder*, set how often you wish to tweet and you're done – until they run out and need to be re-stocked.

3. **Repeat** steps 1 and 2 daily until you are blocked from doing so with the message about Twitter limits. Give it a few hours and hit it again!

   A. Until you break the glass ceiling (2,000 barrier) leave the unfollow function on automatic on *TweetAdder*. You will need to purge almost daily on that section, be sure to check the *"Unfollow any Nonreciprocal Follows"* in the dropdown menu towards the bottom of the page. Also be sure to change the default setting for when to unfollow; you should only wait 1 day for someone to reciprocate (You can be less strict once you've cleared the Glass Ceiling). Make sure that the number of "unfollows" per day keeps up with your growth. If needed, you can even push it through manually. Do this often until your following is equal to or less than your follower count.

B. Once you get past the glass ceiling (2,000 follower)... keep your following count as high as twitter will allow. Jack Thomas, an expert in Twitter building, says, *"if Twitter doesn't stop you from following at least once a day, you aren't really working the system!"*

TIP: The best time of day to follow people, re-tweet etc. and get the most immediate and highest ratio of people that reciprocate is between 4:00 - 6:00 PM Eastern Time (1:00 – 3:00 pm Pacific) and then again at 10:00 PM - 1:00 AM Eastern Time (7:00 - 11:00 PM Pacific)

8

YOU ARE ONLY AS GOOD AS YOUR INFLUENCE
(ALSO SIGNAL, GENEROUSITY, VELOCITY & CLOUT!)

One of the main reasons that you are on Twitter is to develop a base to people that are open to hearing your message, whatever that message may be. This is where I have found that *Twitalyzer* is the most useful for developing your influence over your portion of the Twitterverse. It very quickly tracks your progress (and the progress of others) as well as it is the best and fastest place to learn what the ratings sites feel are important on Twitter. Below are the five categories that *Twitalyzer* uses. If or when *Twitalyzer* falls by the way side, these categories will be very useful in understanding what metrics are used in evaluating your effectiveness, efficiency and reach on Twitter (VERY important):

> ➢ **Influence** is measured by:

- the number of followers you have
- Your relative authority, measured by the number of times you are "re-tweeted"
- Your relative generosity, measured by the number of times you "re-tweet" others
- Your relative clout, measured by the number of times you are referenced by others
- Your relative velocity, measured by the number of updates you publish over a seven day period

➢ **Signal** counts *any update* that includes at least one of the following elements:

- References to other people (defined by the use of "@")
- Links to URLs (defined by the use of "http://" followed by text)
- Hash tags to can explore and participate with (defined by the use of "#")
- Re-tweets of other people, passing along information (defined by the use of "rt", "r/t/", "re-tweet" or "via")

➢ **Generosity** - Being generous with others is good. Thus, generosity is based on the ratio of re-tweets you pass along to all updates you publish.

➢ **Velocity** is the rate at which you contribute to Twitter. Thus set your auto tweets on *TweetAdder* to run every 3 hours. Remember,

that means you will need 8 tweets each day or
56 tweets each week to keep from repeating the
same ones over and over (repeating tweets is
strictly forbidden and WILL get your account
closed)

➢ **Clout** is effected mostly on how often others re-
tweet and mention you

Play around with and get familiar with all of the
different aspects of *Twitalyzer*. The hints and
explanations there will prove valuable to your
developing knowledge as well as your developing
follower base and your influence with them!

No matter what your goal, twitter is a great way to
network, make new friends and associates, and
develop an influence with them. Remember, this
report is intended to get you up and running on
Twitter. The Twitter Blueprint is an integral piece of
the *Social Media Marketing Blueprint*, but it is only one
of the many pieces.

FOOTNOTE

Here is one tip that is very important. If you are recruiting others to your business/cause or selling a product/service, it helps to have a separate page for followers to go to find out more about you, your business/cause and/or your product/service. Post your business links there. This is way, way more effective than just having a link on your twitter page that sends people to your biz. They want to see a little more about you first, before they look at your business. Blogs are good for this. Please keep in mind that SEO works best for blogs and websites. On social media SEO tactics will not only not work, they will fail miserably! SEO and SMO work in tandem.

If you want to get started with a blog, by all means do so! The key isn't really which blogging platform you use, *blogger, wordpress, squidoo – they all have pros and cons.* Devoted fans of each will be happy to fill you in. My recommendation is that when blogging, be consistent and persistent. Create posts at the same interval, no less than once per month – period.

Remember, you don't have to hire a web designer to do effective internet marketing. What is the newest thing? Video is hot, hot, hot! Did I say it's hot? Buy a flip video camera. Record a short video, then post it on Youtube and push onto all the social media platforms as well as your site thus people can get to know you. Remember, this is relationship marketing. People buy you, before they buy your product or opportunity.

ABOUT THE AUTHOR

Anita Fiouris founded *A&A Social Marketing,* a Social Media Management company with her husband, Andreas in 2009. *A&A Social Marketing* offers programs designed to coach, consult or provide full SMO (social media optimization) service to businesses of all types. Anita spends most of her time developing new programs designed to empower others to harness the power we now know as "Social Media". Leaving corporate America in 2007, Anita followed her calling as an entrepreneur. Now she is dedicated to helping others answer their internal pull for business ownership.

Let the non-techy, non-celebrity, social media guru do for you what she did for herself. Her simple, efficient, no nonsense system allows anyone, at any level of technical expertise to run a social media marketing program in less than 90 minutes per week!

Find Anita and her available programs on-line at www.AandASocialMarketing.com; also find her on social media:
 www.Twitter.com/AnitaDFiouris
www.Facebook.com/SocialMktg
www.YouTube.com/AnitaDFiouris
www.BlogTalkRadio.com/EasyLifestyleShow

For a broader understanding of the entire **Social Media Blueprint** visit: **www.SocialMediaA2Z.com** while there watch the most recent interactive online seminar **"Social Marketing Blueprint 101: 5 Simple Steps to Success!"**

www.ingramcontent.com/pod-product-compliance
Lightning Source LLC
Chambersburg PA
CBHW041145050326
40689CB00001B/485

* 9 7 8 1 4 6 0 9 2 6 5 7 4 *